Written on the Sky

Poems from the Japanese

ALSO BY KENNETH REXROTH

SONGS OF LOVE, MOON, & WIND
Poems from the Chinese

Written on the Sky

Poems from the Japanese

Translated by

Kenneth Rexroth

SELECTED BY ELIOT WEINBERGER

A NEW DIRECTIONS BOOK

Cover and Interior Design by **HSU + ASSOCIATES**
Manufactured in the **UNITED STATES OF AMERICA**
New Directions Books are printed on acid-free paper.
First published by New Directions as New Directions Paperbook (NDP1150) in 2009
Published simultaneously in Canada by **PENGUIN BOOKS CANADA LIMITED**

Library of Congress Cataloging-in-Publication Data:

Written on the sky : poems from the Japanese / translated by Kenneth Rexroth ; selected by Eliot Weinberger.
p. cm.
Includes bibliographical references and index.
ISBN 978-0-8112-1837-5 (pbk. : alk. paper)
1. Japanese poetry—Translations into English. 2. Love in literature. I. Rexroth, Kenneth, 1905-1982. II. Weinberger, Eliot.
PL782.E3W73 2009
895.6'1008—dc22

2008050008

NEW DIRECTIONS BOOKS are published for James Laughlin
by New Directions Publishing Corporation
80 Eighth Avenue, New York, NY 10011

TABLE OF CONTENTS

It is the time of rain and snow
I spend sleepless nights
And watch the frost
Frail as your love
Gather in the dawn.

IZUMI SHIKIBU

和泉式部

I think of the days
Before I met her
When I seemed to have
No troubles at all.

FUJIWARA NO ATSUTADA

藤原敦忠

How long will it last?
I do not know
his heart.
This morning my thoughts are as tangled
    with anxiety
as my black hair.

LADY HORIKAWA

堀川女后

The mists rise over
The still pools at Asuka.
Memory does not
Pass away so easily.

YAMABE NO AKAHITO

山部赤人

On Asuka River
Maple leaves are floating.
On Mount Katsuragi,
High upstream, they are
Already falling from the trees.

ANONYMOUS, *MANYŌSHŪ*

作者不詳、万葉集

If I were only sure
I could live as long as I wanted to,
I would not have to weep
at parting from you.

SHIROME

白
女

Who knows
that in the depth of the ravine
of the mountain of my hidden heart
a firefly of my love is aflame.

ABUTSU-NI

阿仏尼

I can no longer tell dream from reality.
Into what world shall I awake
from this bewildering dream?

AKAZOME EMON

赤染衛門

How beautiful the Buddhist statues
At Saga
Half hidden in falling leaves.

IMAIZUMI SOGETSU-NI

今泉素月尼

The flowers whirl away
In the wind like snow.
The thing that falls away
Is myself.

PRIME MINISTER KINTSUNE

太政大臣公経

Frozen in the ice
A maple leaf.

MASAOKA SHIKI

正岡子規

The Spring night's
Floating bridge of dreams
Breaks off. The clouds banked
Against the mountain peak
Dissipate in the clear sky.

FUJIWARA NO TEIKA

藤原定家

The pillow that knows all
won't tell, for it doesn't know,
and don't you tell
of our dream of a Spring night.

IZUMI SHIKIBU

和泉式部

I went out in the Spring
To gather the young herbs.
So many petals were falling
Drifting in confused flight
That I lost my way.

KI NO TSURAYUKI

紀貫之

Others may forget you, but not I.
I am haunted by your beautiful ghost.

EMPRESS YAMATOHIME

倭姫命

My hunter of dragonflies,
How far
has he wandered today?

FUKUDA CHIYO-NI

福田千代尼

Will I cease to be,
Or will I remember
Beyond the world,
Our last meeting together?

IZUMI SHIKIBU

和泉式部

Everyone is asleep
There is nothing to come between
the moon and me.

ENOMOTO SEIFU-JO

榎本星布女

No, the human heart
Is unknowable.
But in my birthplace
The flowers still smell
The same as always.

KI NO TSURAYUKI

紀貫之

I was sure I would never get lost
in the tangled roads of love.
Now I have been caught
in the karma of past lives.

KENREI MON-IN UKYŌ NO DAIBU

建礼門院右京大夫

The fireflies' light.
How easily it goes on
How easily it goes out again.

CHINE-JO

千子女

I sit at home
In our room
By our bed
Gazing at your pillow.

KAKINOMOTO NO HITOMARO

柿本人麿

I fell asleep thinking of him,
and he came to me.
If I had known it was only a dream
I would never have awakened.

ONO NO KOMACHI

小野小町

We were together
Only a little while,
And we believed our love
Would last a thousand years.

ŌTOMO NO YAKAMOCHI

大伴家持

That evening when
You went away the two of
Us wrote together
On a pillar a poem
About a white clover.

YOSANO AKIKO

与謝野晶子

Shall we stay in the
House to make love, when over
The grasses of Inami Moor
There glows the moonfilled night?

ANONYMOUS, *MANYŌSHŪ*

作者不詳、万葉集

We dressed each other
Hurrying to say farewell
In the depth of night.
Our drowsy thighs touched and we
Were caught in bed by the dawn.

EMPRESS EIFUKU

永福門院

The white chrysanthemum
Is disguised by the first frost.
If I wanted to pick one
I could find it only by chance.

ŌSHIKOCHI NO MITSUNE

凡河躬恒

Involuntary,
I may live on
In the passing world,
Never forgetting
This midnight moon.

EMPEROR SANJŌ

三条天皇

You say, “I will come.”
And you do not come.
Now you say, “I will not come.”
So I shall expect you.
Have I learned to understand you?

LADY ŌTOMO NO SAKANOE

大伴坂上郎女

Better never to have met you
In my dream
Than to wake and reach
For hands that are not there.

ŌTOMO NO YAKAMOCHI

大伴家持

Do not smile to yourself
Like a green mountain
With a cloud drifting across it.
People will know we are in love.

LADY ŌTOMO NO SAKANOE

大伴坂上郎女

How can I blame the cherry blossoms
for rejecting this floating world
and drifting away as the wind calls them?

SHUNZEI'S DAUGHTER

藤原俊成之女

I go out of the darkness
Onto a road of darkness
Lit only by the far off
Moon on the edge of the mountains.

IZUMI SHIKIBU

和泉式部

I gaze far and long,
Not at cherry blossoms,
Not at Autumn leaves,
But at only a thatched hut,
By an inlet,
In the Autumn dusk.

FUJIWARA NO TEIKA

藤原定家

The cicada cries out
Burning with love.
The firefly burns
With silent love.

ANONYMOUS

作者不詳

The leaves of the bush clover rustle in the
wind.
I, not a leaf,
watched you without a sound.
You may have thought I paid no attention.

KENREI MON-IN UKYŌ NO DAIBU

建礼門院右京大夫

When I went out in
The Spring fields to pick
The young greens for you
Snow fell on my sleeves.

EMPEROR KŌKŌ

光孝天皇

The deer on pine mountain,
Where there are no falling leaves,
Knows the coming of Autumn
Only by the sound of his own voice.

ŌNAKATOMI NO YOSHINOBU

大中臣能宣

I can see the stones
On the bottom fluctuate
Through the clear water.

MASAOKA SHIKI

正岡子規

In the Autumn mountains
The colored leaves are falling.
If I could hold them back,
I could still see her.

KAKINOMOTO NO HITOMARO

柿本人麿

The hanging raindrops
Have not dried from the needles
Of the fir forest
Before the evening mist
Of Autumn rises.

MONK JAKUREN

寂蓮法師

The colored leaves
Have hidden the paths
On the Autumn mountain.
How can I find my girl,
Wandering on ways I do not know?

KAKINOMOTO NO HITOMARO

柿本人麿

A strange old man
Stops me,
Looking out of my deep mirror.

KAKINOMOTO NO HITOMARO

柿本人麿

I should not have waited.
It would have been better
To have slept and dreamed,
Than to have watched night pass,
And this slow moon sink.

AKAZOME EMON

赤染衛門

I may live on until
I long for this time
In which I am so unhappy,
And remember it fondly.

FUJIWARA NO KIYOSUKE

藤原清輔

Evening darkens until
I can no longer see the path.
Still I find my way home,
My horse has gone this way before.

ANONYMOUS, *GOSENSHŪ*

作者不詳、

後撰集

In the Summer, by the river,
Let us sit in the evening
And watch the lights of the boats
Caught and confused
In a net of fireflies.

ANONYMOUS

作者不詳

In the eternal
Light of the Spring day
The flowers fall away
Like the unquiet heart.

KI NO TOMONORI

紀
友
則

No one spoke,
The host, the guest,
The white chrysanthemums.

ŌSHIMA RYŌTA

大島蓼太

An old pond—
The sound
Of a diving frog.

MATSUO BASHŌ

松尾芭蕉

The tree from whose flower
This perfume comes
Is unknowable.

MATSUO BASHŌ

松尾芭蕉

All day I hoe weeds.
At night I sleep.
All night I hoe again
In dreams the weeds of the day.

ANONYMOUS

作者不詳

The first time I saw you
Was last year in May,
In May, bathing in a pool
Crowded with iris.

ANONYMOUS

作者不詳

Everybody knows
How much I love you.
All your
Mannerisms
Have become my
Mannerisms.

ANONYMOUS

作者不詳

Although I hide it
My love shows in my face
So plainly that he asks me,
"Are you thinking of something?"

TAIRA NO KANEMORI

平清盛

The purity of the moonlight,
Falling out of the immense sky,
Is so great that it freezes
The water touched by its rays.

ANONYMOUS

作者不詳

The crying plovers
On darkening Narumi
Beach, grow closer, wing
To wing, as the moon declines
Behind the rising tide.

FUJIWARA NO SUEYOSHI

藤原季能

I feel of others' affairs
as though they were
the water birds I watch
floating idly on the water.
My idleness comes
only from sorrow.

MURASAKI SHIKIBU

紫式部

The first dawn comes
With a clear bright flicker and
You must go. In the early morning,
We help each other to dress
Trembling with sorrow.

ANONYMOUS

作者不詳

Everybody tells me
My hair is too long
I leave it
As you saw it last
Dishevelled by your hands.

LADY SONO NO OMI IKUHA

園臣生羽之女

In a gust of wind the white dew
On the Autumn grass
Scatters like a broken necklace.

BUNYA NO ASAYASU

文屋朝康

I slept in the past,
that will never come back,
as though it was the present.
Around my pillow in my dreams
the perfume of orange blossoms floated,
like the fragrance of the sleeves
of the man who is gone.

PRINCESS SHIKISHI

式子内親王

I loathe the twin seas
Of being and not being
And long for the mountain
Of bliss untouched by
The changing tides.

ANONYMOUS, *MANYŌSHŪ*

作者不詳、

万葉集

The Autumn cicada
Dies beside its shell.

NAITŌ JŌSŌ

内藤丈草

Whenever the wind blows
I try to question it,
although it has obliterated
the spider's web against the sky.

MOTHER OF MICHITSUNA

道綱の母

I passed by the beach
At Tago and saw
The snow falling, pure white,
High on the peak of Fuji.

YAMABE NO AKAHITO

山部赤人

At Ichiyiama
Boating on Lake Nio
The moon and fireflies
To the right and left.

MATSUMOTO KOYŪ-NI

松本古友尼

On the road through the clouds
Is there a shortcut
To the Summer moon?

DEN SUTE-JO

田捨女

I have always known
That at last I would
Take this road, but yesterday
I did not know that it would be today.

ARIWARA NO NARIHIRA

在原業平

The moon is full
The night is very still
My heart beats
Like a bell.

ANONYMOUS, *MANYŌSHŪ*

作者不詳、万葉集

Why should I be bitter
About someone who was
A complete stranger
Until a certain moment
In a day that has passed.

SAIGYŌ

西行法師

I cannot go to you
Even in dreams
For in my breast
The skies are overcast
And my mind is clouded.

ANONYMOUS, *GOSENSHŪ*

作者不詳、 後撰集

In the mountain village
The wind rustles the leaves.
Deep in the night, the deer
Cry out beyond the edge of dreams.

MINAMOTO NO MOROTADA

源師忠

We are, you and me,
Like two pine needles
Which will dry and fall
But never separate.

ANONYMOUS

作者不詳

My heart, like my clothing
is saturated with your fragrance.
Your vows of fidelity
were made to our pillow and not to me.

KENREI MON-IN UKYŌ NO DAIBU

建礼門院右京大夫

May those who are born after me
Never travel such roads of love.

KAKINOMOTO NO HITOMARO

柿本人麿

Only the waning morning moon
visits my garden
where no lover comes.

ISE TAYŪ

伊勢大輔

This life of ours would not cause you
sorrow
if you thought of it as like
the mountain cherry blossoms
which bloom and fade in a day.

MURASAKI SHIKIBU

紫式部

Wild goose, wild goose,
At what age
Did you make your first journey?

ISSA

一
茶

Out in the marsh reeds
A bird cries out in sorrow,
As though it had recalled
Something better forgotten.

KI NO TSURAYUKI

紀貫之

In all the world
There is no way whatever.
The stag cries even
In the most remote mountain.

FUJIWARA NO TOSHINARI

藤原俊成

The snow falls and falls.
The mountains and meadows sleep.
Only an old mill
Stays awake.

ŌKURA ICHIJITSU

大倉一実

If only the world
Would always remain this way,
Some fishermen
Drawing a little rowboat
Up the riverbank.

MINAMOTO NO SANETOMO

源
実
朝

Following the roads
Of dream to you, my feet
Never rest. But one glimpse of you
In reality would be
Worth all these many nights of love.

ONO NO KOMACHI

小野小町

In the dusk
The road is hard to see.
Wait till moonrise,
So I can watch you go.

ŌYAKE-ME

豊前國娘子

From the North send a message
on the wings of the wild geese,
written again and again
by their flight across the clouds.

MURASAKI SHIKIBU

紫式部

I will come to you
Through the ford at Saho,
The plovers piping about me
As my horse wades
The clear water.

ŌTOMO NO YAKAMOCHI

大伴家持

INDEX

[*Women poets are noted with an *.*]